INDIAN
•SIGN•
LANGUAGE

INDIAN
•SIGN•
LANGUAGE

ROBERT HOFSINDE
(GRAY-WOLF)

SCHOLASTIC INC.
New York Toronto London Auckland Sydney

To

the American Indian

of Yesterday, Today,

and Tomorrow.

ISBN 0-590-38193-8

12 11 10 9 8 7 6 5 4 3   7 8 9/9 0 1 2/0

Printed in the U.S.A.   40
First Scholastic printing, October 1997

The author wishes to express his appreciation to the many people throughout the United States who, for many years, have worked with him and his wife to help preserve American Indian lore for today's children. He is especially grateful to Mr. and Mrs. Willard L. Kauth, the directors of the Boys' Athletic League and the Girls' Vacation Fund, whose untiring interest in Indian life has made Indian dance groups, crafts, sign language, and legends an integral part of the organizations' summer camp programs.

The author also wishes to acknowledge his indebtedness to Chief Blow Snake of the Winnebago tribe and the late Chief Crazy Bull of the Sioux, who verified many signs for him, and to Dr. John P. Harrington, Ethnologist of the Smithsonian Institution, who read and criticized the manuscript.

A soft breeze carries the sounds of familiar evening activities through the Blackfeet village. The dull clop-clop of an unshod pony as it is ridden through the camp mingles with the distant sound of a medicine song, chanted to the pulsating throb of a tom-tom. There is a murmur of voices and laughter, and the barking of dogs. The fragrant smoke of many lodge fires fills the air.

Silence surrounds one of the largest tepees; it seems deserted except for the glow of firelight inside it. This is the council lodge. Behind its skin door covering, the magnificently dressed representatives of the Crow, Sioux, Cheyenne, Arapaho, and Kiowa Indians are seated round the fire with their Blackfeet

7

hosts. The pipe has been passed around. There is a ripple of spoken words in six tribal languages, each as different from the other as French is from English.

Wolf Robe, a Blackfeet, raises his hand for attention. With graceful motions of the hands and fingers, he begins to address the gathering in the Indian sign language. Although his spoken words would be foreign to his listeners, they understand him perfectly. Sign talk is used and understood by all the Indian tribes.

No one can be sure just how ancient the Indians' system of sign language is, but we do know that it was practiced among American Indian tribes for centuries before the white man arrived. Like the war bonnet, it reached its greatest development among the Plains Indians. These Indians were wanderers, never camping long in any one place. When two tribes met on the trail, or hunted buffalo together, there was not enough time to learn each other's spoken language. Sign language took its place. Just as Latin was the universal language of all the peoples of Europe during the Middle Ages, sign language was the universal language of the American Indian tribes.

The first white adventurers, trappers and mountain men, soon learned the value of sign talk in dealing with the Indians. By learning it, they could move freely from tribe to tribe and always be certain they could make themselves understood. The white men brought with them many things that were new and strange to the Indian. Soon signs for these white-man things—such as bacon, coffee, calico—were added to the Indians' sign language.

We know that our own language varies slightly in different regions; the name for something in one part of the country may be pronounced differently in another section. This is also true of Indian sign language. Certain signs changed form among some *of the tribes, but in most cases the difference is a slight one. Most of the signs described in this book are easily understood among all tribes.*

For the Indians of yesterday, sign language was a necessity; for American boys and girls of today sign language is fun. It is useful, too. Whenever it is convenient to talk silently—on nature hikes, for instance—sign language is a great help. By practicing it and using it among your friends, you can soon develop great skill in an ancient art that is still used by the American Indian.

MAN   Hold right hand in front of chest, index finger pointing up, and raise it in front of face. Also **MALE**.

WOMAN   With fingers of both hands slightly curved, make downward motions from top of head to shoulders, as if combing long hair. Also **FEMALE**.

FATHER   Touch right side of chest with closed right hand several times.

MOTHER   Touch left side of chest in same way as for **FATHER**.

BROTHER   Touch lips with index and second fingers, and move hand straight out from mouth. Then sign **MAN**. Also **PARTNER**.

SISTER   Sign **WOMAN**. Then touch lips and move hand as for **BROTHER**.

BOY Sign MAN, and indicate boy's height with flat right hand.

GIRL Sign WOMAN, and indicate height, as above.

ALL Move flat right hand in a horizontal circle, clockwise, in front of chest.

I (ME) Point to self with right thumb.

YOU Point to person with right thumb.

HE (HIM) **SHE (HER)** { If person is present, point to him or her; if person is not present, sign MAN or WOMAN.

THEY (THEM) **WE (US)** { Point to persons, and sign ALL.

MY (MINE) **HIS (HERS)** **YOURS** **OURS** **THEIRS** Hold right hand in front of neck, thumb up, and move it two or three inches forward, turning the wrist so the thumb points to the person or persons you wish to indicate. Also OWN, GET, HAVE.

MIND Touch forehead with index and second finger of right hand.

FRIEND Hold hand as shown, then raise it to the side of the face. *Meaning:* Growing up together. Some Indian tribes make the sign for friend by shaking their own hands.

TRADE With the index fingers pointing up, raise both hands and quickly move them past each other, ending sign in position shown. Also SELL, EXCHANGE.

MARRY Sign TRADE, and hold index fingers side by side as shown.

HUSBAND Sign MAN and MARRY.

WIFE Sign WOMAN and MARRY.

FATHER-IN-LAW Sign WIFE or HUSBAND, as the case may be, and FATHER.

MOTHER-IN-LAW Same as above, ending with sign for MOTHER.

NEAR (CLOSE) Hold left arm as shown, fingers curved slightly. Then bring hand in until tips of fingers touch shoulder.

FAR (DISTANT) Reverse of CLOSE. Start at shoulder and bring hand out to curved position. If showing great distance, extend arm to full length.

RELATIVE (KIN) Sign BROTHER. Then sign either NEAR or FAR, depending upon relationship.

OLD Bend body slightly forward, and extend right hand as if leaning on a staff. Move hand up and down, while holding left hand on back above hip.

STEAL Hold left hand open, palm toward body, and draw closed right hand, with index finger crooked, under left hand. Close index finger of right hand as it touches body. Also LOST, HIDE, CONCEAL, ASTRAY.

NO Hold right hand in front of body, fingers pointing to left. Swing arm to right so palm shows, and return hand to starting position.

ELOPE Sign STEAL and WOMAN.

BACHELOR Sign MAN, NO, and MARRY.

GRANDFATHER (GRANDMOTHER) Sign FATHER or MOTHER, and OLD.

AUNT Sign FATHER and SISTER, or MOTHER and SISTER.

BABY Rest fist of right hand in bend of left arm, holding left hand open as shown. Then rock arms slightly, as if holding a baby.

ABANDON Hold hands as shown and drop them toward hips with a downward motion, opening them as if throwing something behind you.

14

PEOPLE Hold both hands in front of shoulders, fingers spread and pointing up. Move hands together and apart a few times, by wrist action.

SON (DAUGHTER) Sign BOY or GIRL, RELATIVE, and NEAR.

BROTHER-IN-LAW Cross right arm over left at wrists so arms are flat against chest, fingers extended. Then strike the extended right hand downward past left elbow.

SISTER-IN-LAW Sign BROTHER, HIS, and WIFE.

DIVORCE Sign HIS, WOMAN, and ABANDON.

YES Place right hand even with shoulder, index finger pointing straight up, thumb pressing on second finger. Then quickly drop hand downward, closing index finger over end of thumb.

TIME Hold hands as shown, index fingers pointing. Draw right hand back about two inches.

BEFORE Position as above, but draw right hand back several inches. Also LONG TIME—PAST, AHEAD.

AFTER Sign TIME, then move right hand past and ahead of left. Also LONG TIME—FUTURE, SINCE.

JEALOUS Close fists in front of body, arms rigid and elbows out. Move right elbow to right and back a little. Repeat with left arm. Alternate this motion a few times, as if elbowing someone to one side.

ANCESTOR Sign OLD and PEOPLE. Some Indians add BEFORE to these two signs.

NIGHT Hold both hands horizontally, palms down in front of body and several inches apart. Slowly fold arms across chest until right arm rests on top of left.

16

DAY With arms folded, as in NIGHT, raise both hands until fingers point skyward. Also **LIGHT**.

SUNRISE Hold right hand across left side of chest, thumb and index finger making an incomplete circle, and raise it even with shoulder.

SUNSET Sign SUNRISE in reverse.

DAYBREAK Place hands in front of chest, palms in and fingers together, with little finger of right hand resting on index finger of left hand. Raise right hand about two inches.

MORNING Sign DAY and SUNRISE.

LIGHTNING Describe zigzag in air with right index finger.

NOW Hold right hand several inches in front of face, index finger pointing up, and snap wrist in a few whiplike motions. Also **TODAY**.

MIDDLE Hold closed left hand at chest level, with index finger pointing to right. Then, from above, point to middle joint of left index finger with right index finger.

LITTLE Hold right hand even with shoulder, as shown, with thumbnail touching ball of index finger.

BIG Hold both hands in front of body, with palms facing each other, and move them apart. Also WIDE.

EARLY Sign DAY and LITTLE.

MIDNIGHT Sign NIGHT and MIDDLE

NOON Form incomplete circle with thumb and index finger of right hand, and hold hand over head. Also MIDDAY.

MEDICINE (meaning anything mysterious, unknown, or of the spirit) Hold hand as shown and move it upward in a spiral.

MEDICINE MAN Sign MAN and MEDICINE.

SUNDAY Sign DAY and MEDICINE. Other days in the week are described by signing the number of days before or after Medicine Day plus the sign for BEFORE or AFTER. *For example:*

    FRIDAY Sign TWO, DAY, BEFORE, and SUNDAY.

    TUESDAY Sign TWO, DAY, AFTER, and SUNDAY.

YESTERDAY Sign NIGHT. Move right hand upward and to the right from overlapped position, turning palm up.

GOOD Hold right hand, palm down, thumb close to left breast. Then, keeping arm horizontal, sweep hand outward and a little to the right. *Meaning:* Level with the heart.

SUN Hold thumb and index finger of right hand in incomplete circle, with hand to left. Then move hand upward to the right. Left indicates the east; right, the west.

EVENING Sign SUN, holding hand to right instead of left. Then sign NIGHT and LITTLE.

BAD Hold clenched right fist in front of body, and sweep down to the right, at the same time opening hand as if throwing something away.

SNOW Lift both hands even with shoulders, hands hanging loosely at wrists, fingers spread. Then move hands downward in a spiral movement (see diagram).

WINTER Hold fists in front of chest, as shown. Shake them as if shivering from the cold. Also AGE.

COLD Same as above.

YEAR Sign WINTER. For this year, add NOW; for last year, add BEFORE.

GRASS Hold hands near ground, fingers curved upward and slightly apart. Then swing hands out in a slight upward curve

HIGH Hold right hand, palm down, even with shoulder, and raise or lower to show height.

SPRING Sign GRASS and LITTLE.

SUMMER Sign GRASS and HIGH.

DRUM Hold index finger and thumb of left hand in semi-circle, and make drumming motions on it with closed right hand.

RAIN Hold closed fists in front of shoulders, as shown, and lower them slowly, opening fingers at the same time. Repeat sign a few times.

DROUGHT Sign BEFORE, NO, and RAIN.

ALWAYS Hold palm of hand close to right ear and, with wrist action, move it back and forth slightly. Also FOREVER.

END Hold open left hand in front of body. Then, with open right hand, strike down past finger tips of left hand. Also CUT OFF, FINISHED, DONE.

BEYOND Hold both hands open in front of body, palms down, and swing the right hand across and down past the left hand, at the same time turning right hand so palm is up.

22

TREE Hold left hand open in front of shoulder, fingers spread. Then raise hand slowly upward to indicate growth.

LEAF Sign TREE with left hand, holding right hand as shown. Shake right hand several times, like a leaf in a breeze.

MANY (MUCH) Raise hands in front of body, fingers slightly curved. Then sweep hands together in a looping curve, as in diagram. Also **PLENTY**.

FOREST Raise both hands above head, fingers spread, and shake them slightly. Add sign for MANY.

SLEEP Rest head on fingers of left hand in palm of right hand.

AUTUMN Sign TREE and LEAF, and move right hand downward slowly in a fluttering motion.

QUESTION Hold right hand, palm out, even with shoulder. Rotate hand slightly a few times. The sign for QUESTION always precedes the sentence.

HOW MANY? Sign QUESTION, then strike right index finger against each finger of the left hand in quick succession. Close fingers of left hand as they are struck.

WHEN? Sign QUESTION, and SLEEP (day), or MOON (month), or WINTER (year).

WHERE? Sign QUESTION and point in all directions.

WATER Cup hand and raise to mouth as if drinking from it. Also **DRINK**.

RIVER Sign WATER. Then place right hand across face, index finger extended, and draw it to right until it is even with the right shoulder.

BROOK Sign RIVER and LITTLE.

LAKE Sign WATER. Then form a horizontal circle with thumbs and index fingers of both hands to indicate shore line.

OCEAN Sign WATER and BIG.

SWIM Sign WATER, and make motions of swimming.

OFTEN With index finger of right hand, strike left forearm several times, from wrist to elbow. Also **MANY TIMES.**

FEW Hold both hands in front of body about eight inches apart, with the right higher than the left and the palms facing each other. Then move them together, ending the sign with the finger tips of the left hand touching the heel of the right hand. Also **NARROW.**

ISLAND Make incomplete circle with fingers, as for LAKE, and sign WATER with right hand. With left hand still in "circle" position, draw an imaginary circle with the right hand.

FISH Sign WATER, and move right hand forward from hip in a waving motion.

FOG Sign WATER, and cross open hands, with backs out, in front of face.

FROG Sign WATER and, with bunched right hand, show motion of frog jumping.

HOLD Place hands in front of chest, backs out and fingers overlapping. Move arms from side to side in rocking motion.

DAM Sign RIVER and HOLD.

HARD Strike palm of left hand with right fist several times.

SOFT Sign HARD and NO.

STONE Sign HARD, and indicate shape of rock or stone. Also ROCK.

FREEZE Sign COLD, WATER, and HARD.

FREEZE OVER Sign COLD, WATER, and RIVER. Then hold both hands even with shoulders, backs up and fingers pointing forward, and move them together slowly until index fingers touch.

ICE Sign WATER, COLD, and FREEZE OVER.

RAPIDS Sign RIVER and STONE. Then with right hand held chest high, fingers extended, move it forward and down with a waving motion.

WALK Hold hands flat and move them forward alternately as if walking. If referring to an animal, close hands into fists and repeat same motion.

RUN Sign WALK and FAST.

LOOK (SEE) Hold right hand just below right eye, index and second fingers slightly parted and pointing ahead. Also HUNT.

GO Hold flat right hand in front of body, and move it forward about a foot, ending the sign in a slight upward curve. Also **START, DEPART**.

GONE Sign GO and BEFORE.

EARTH Point to ground with right index finger and reach down. Then rub thumb against tips of first two fingers of right hand. Also **DIRT**.

TRACK Sign WALK, and point to the ground.

TRAIL Sign TRACK and LOOK.

FOOTPRINT Sign WALK and LOOK, turning spread fingers toward ground.

MOUNTAIN Raise closed right fist straight up past side of head, and sign HARD. Then make zigzag line to show outline of mountains.

HILL Sign MOUNTAIN and LITTLE.

PRAIRIE Hold both hands under chin, palms up, and little fingers touching. Then move hands straight apart.

CORN Grasp thumb and index finger of left hand with thumb and index of right, and twist right hand several times.

MAKE (WORK) Place hands, palms facing each other, a few inches apart in front of body. Move hands up and down past each other. Also DO.

DO NOT Sign MAKE and NO.

PLANT Sign CORN and MAKE.

BLANKET Hold both hands even with shoulders, and bring them forward across chest, as if wrapping one's self in a blanket. Also ROBE.

WOLF Rest middle fingers of right hand on right thumb, extending index and little finger. This shows the pointed snout and ears of the wolf. Also CUNNING, SPY.

COYOTE Sign WOLF and LITTLE.

BIRD Move hands up and down in flight motion. Slow motion indicates big birds; very fast motion, small birds.

HORSE Hold left hand, palm in, in front of chest, and place index and second finger of right hand astride edge of left hand.

PONY Sign HORSE and LITTLE.

RIDE Sign HORSE, and rotate hands in small circles, as if trotting. Also ASTRIDE.

BEAVER Hold hands, palms down, in front of body, right hand below left, and strike back of right hand sharply against left palm.

TAIL (of a bird) Hold right hand, fingers spread, at base of spine.

TAIL (of an animal) Same position as above, but hand is closed, with only index finger pointing down.

BUFFALO Hold hands, backs forward, against ears, as shown. Curved index fingers indicate horns, and extended thumbs are ears. Wiggle "ears" slightly, as animals do when listening.

BUFFALO CALF Sign BUFFALO, without "horns."

BUFFALO ROBE Sign BUFFALO and BLANKET.

CAT Tilt tip of nose up with right thumb and index finger, and show size of animal.

DOG Draw index and second finger of right hand in front of body, to indicate dog drawing travois poles. If you are seated, draw fingers across ground in same way.

DEER Hold hands, backs out, against sides of head, with fingers spread to indicate antlers.

ELK Same as DEER, but hold hands higher, and move them forward and back a few times to indicate large antlers.

COLOR Rub center of left palm with index and second finger of right hand in small circular motion. To sign any color except red, point to an object of that color and make above sign.

RED Rub right cheek with tips of fingers on right hand. Red is the only color for which there is a specific sign.

EAGLE Extend left hand in front of body, back up. Place right hand across left hand so the little finger rests on the knuckles of left hand, and swing right hand to the right.

CHICKEN Sign BIRD and RED. Then place heel of right hand along top of head, and spread fingers to indicate cock's comb.

OWL Sign BIRD, and circle eyes with fingers.

SPOTTED Hold left arm in front of body, and flick finger tips of right hand back and forth along left arm from wrist to elbow.

CATTLE (COW) Sign BUFFALO and SPOTTED.

STRIPED Hold left arm in front of body, and stroke across it with the palm of the right hand from wrist to elbow.

BEAR Cup both hands around ears to show rounded ears of bear. Then make clawing motions downward with both hands.

FEATHER (worn as decoration) Sign BIRD. Then hold raised index finger at back of head. Some tribes add sign for TAIL.

CLOUD Curve open hands above head, and swing them down to shoulders.

GLOOMY Curve open hands above head, and swing them down in front of face.

FRAGRANT Hold right hand in front of chin and move index and second finger up to either side of nose, as shown. Then sign GOOD.

SMELL (ODOR) Same as above, without sign for GOOD.

HEAR Hold right hand behind ear. Also LISTEN.

LAND Lower both hands, palms down, toward ground, and spread them apart horizontally.

TAKE Point right index finger and move hand forward. Then pull hand back, hooking index finger at the same time. Also CATCH.

DIE Hold left hand open in front of body, and point right index finger at left palm. Jab index finger toward palm but, at last moment, dip right hand under left. *Meaning:* Going under.

DEAD Sign DIE and SLEEP.

MILKY WAY The Indians believed that the Milky Way, or Wolf Trail, was the path to the Happy Hunting Grounds, or Sand Hills, after death. Either of two signs are used. The Sioux sign: DIE and TRAIL. The Blackfeet sign: DIE, TAKE, WOLF, and TRAIL. In both cases the sign ends in a sweeping gesture.

STAR Sign NIGHT. Then form a small circle with thumb and index finger of right hand, raising it toward the sky. To indicate a bright star, sign TWINKLE by snapping index finger forward from thumb a few times.

WIND Hold both hands, palms down, in front of body, and move in wavy motions to show direction of the wind.

SNAKE Hold right hand near hip, index finger pointing ahead, and move hand forward about one foot in a snaky motion.

RATTLESNAKE Sign SNAKE. Then raise right index finger and shake it hard.

GROW Hold right hand near ground, with index finger pointing up. Move it upward in short jerks until it is even with face.

SADDLE Place heels of hands together in front of chest.

CAPTIVE (PRISONER) Close fists, and place right hand over left at wrists as if they were bound together.

ESCAPE Hold hands as above. Then separate hands quickly as if breaking bonds, and sign GO.

TALK Place back of right hand against chin, with index finger and thumb forming circle. Then snap index finger forward without moving hand, and repeat. Also SPEAK.

SING Sign TALK, but as index finger snaps forward, carry hand up in spiral.

SCOLD Sign TALK and BAD.

BOOK Place palms of hands together, and open them, as if opening a book.

READ Sign BOOK and LOOK.

SECRET Shape circle of index finger and thumb of right hand as in TALK, holding hand in front of chest. Shield right hand under palm of left hand and snap index finger forward a few times.

SIT Hold closed right hand a little below shoulder, and bring downward a few inches in a short, quick motion. Also STAY, HERE.

BOW Hold left hand forward, as if grasping a bow, and draw right hand back, as if pulling arrow on bowstring.

SHOOT Sign BOW, and snap right hand open as if releasing arrow.

ARROW Draw right index finger from closed left hand, as if drawing arrow from bundle of arrows usually held in left hand while hunting.

ENEMY Sign FRIEND and NO.

WAR BONNET Raise open hands, palms forward, at each side of head, fingers well spread. Then move hands back and out to show spread of bonnet.

WARRIOR Sign MAN and WAR.

INDIAN Rub back of left hand from wrist to knuckle with right index finger.

SCOUT Sign INDIAN and WOLF.

Common Indian Tribes

APACHE Sign INDIAN, and slide right index finger down left index finger from tip to knuckle two or three times.

SIOUX (Cutthroat) Draw the right index finger across the neck with a slashing motion. Sign INDIAN.

PAWNEE (Wolf) Sign WOLF and INDIAN.

COMANCHE (Snake) Sign INDIAN and SNAKE.

BLACKFEET Sign BLACK, COLOR, and MOCCASINS, or point to foot. Then sign INDIAN.

CHIPPEWA (OJIBWAY) Fold fingers of left hand over palm, and push fingers of right hand under them to indicate the puckered moccasins worn by this tribe. Sign INDIAN.

OSAGE (Shaved head) Hold both hands, palms out, as shown, at back of head. Move the hands downward as if shaving off hair with edge of hands, and repeat. Sign INDIAN.

NAVAJO Sign INDIAN, WORK, BLANKET, and STRIPED.

UTE Sign INDIAN, BLACK, COLOR, and RED.

SHOSHONE (Sheep eater) Sign INDIAN, MOUNTAIN SHEEP, and EAT.

CROW Place back of closed right fist against forehead, to indicate hair style used by this tribe. Sometimes signed BIRD, BLACK, COLOR, and INDIAN.

NEZ PERCÉ (Pierced nose)   Slide right index finger from right to left under the nose, and sign INDIAN.

SOUTHERN ARAPAHO   Rub right-hand side of nose with right index finger, holding hand palm outward, and sign INDIAN.

NORTHERN ARAPAHO   This tribe considered itself the "mother" of all tribes. Sign MOTHER, ALL, and INDIAN.

CHEYENNE   Draw right index finger across left index finger from knuckle to tip as if cutting. This sign refers to the Cheyenne fondness for striped arrow feathers. Sign INDIAN.

DANCE Hold hands about eight inches apart, palms facing each other and fingers pointing up, and move them up and down alternately, in short, jerky motions.

WAR DANCE Sign WAR and DANCE.

SIGN LANGUAGE Hold both hands flat in front of body, a little below the chest. Rub back of left hand against the right hand, then right against left. Repeat motion several times, and sign TALK.

BRAVE (STRONG) Hold right fist above left fist in front of body, and strike right hand downward past left hand.

CHIEF With index finger pointing up, raise right hand in an arc above face. *Meaning:* One who stands above his people.

FAME Sign CHIEF and BRAVE.

AMONG Hold left hand in front of chest, with fingers spread, and poke right index finger between fingers of left hand.

TEPEE Cross index fingers in front of face, and draw hands downward and apart to describe the sloping walls of a tepee. Also **LODGE**.

INSIDE (in my tepee) Sign TEPEE and SIT.

VILLAGE (CAMP) Sign TEPEE, and make circle with thumbs and index fingers to show group of lodges. Some tribes sign TEPEE and MANY.

45

FIGHT (WAR) Make motions of shadow boxing.

PRAY Sign MAKE and MEDICINE.

LUCK Sign GOOD or BAD, and MEDICINE. Also **GOOD MEDICINE, BAD MEDICINE.**

TOBACCO Place closed right hand in left palm and move it in a circular motion, as if grinding tobacco leaves.

PIPE Place hands in front of body, as if holding long-stemmed pipe, and move them forward and back slightly, as if removing and returning pipe to mouth.

SMOKE (pipe smoke) Strike left fist with open right hand, and sign PIPE.

FIRE Cup right hand close to ground, fingers partly closed, and raise it a few inches in a wavy motion.

SMOKE (wood smoke) Sign FIRE, and continue to raise the hand to show smoke curling upward.

CAMPFIRE Sign FIRE, SIT, and TALK.

NAME Place back of closed right hand against mouth, with thumb and index finger together. Then move hand forward about one inch, at the same time pointing index finger toward person. To say "What is your name?" sign QUESTION and NAME.

PRIEST Move both hands from shoulders to below the knees to indicate a long robe, and sign BLACK.

PAINT Rub the cheek and forehead with the open hand, as if applying war paint.

47

TOMAHAWK Rest right elbow in palm of left hand, right hand even with left shoulder, and chop downward with right hand. Also AX.

HATCHET Sign TOMAHAWK and LITTLE.

PARTS OF DRESS Spread thumb and index finger and pass them over item of dress in question. *For example:*

MOCCASINS Pass spread thumbs and index fingers over feet from toes to ankles.

LEGGINGS Pass spread thumbs and index fingers over legs from ankles to top of thighs.

PARTS OF THE BODY Point to part of body you wish to indicate. *For example:*

HAIR Point to your own hair.

BALD Sign HAIR and DESTROY, or NO.

RATTLE Shake closed right hand, as if holding a rattle.

MIRROR Hold open right hand in front of face, palm in, and turn face slightly from side to side as if looking into mirror.

DREAM Sign SLEEP, SEE, and GOOD.

SMALL If showing size of an animal, person, or object, indicate its height with open right hand. For a small amount of something, sign FEW.

KNIFE Place left fist in front of mouth and slice between it and the face with edge of open right hand. This sign grew out of the early custom of eating meat by holding a piece in the teeth and slicing off a bite.

DULL Rub edge of open right hand across left palm several times, and sign BAD.

SHARP Hold open left hand, palm up, in front of chest, and gently touch edge of hand with right thumb, as if testing a knife edge. Then sign GOOD.

COUNCIL Hold both fists together in front of chest, with backs of hands out. Separate hands, swinging them in a circle until they come together, thumb to thumb, close to chest. Then sign TALK to left and to right.

ARRIVE HERE Hold left hand open, back out, in front of shoulder. Point to it with right index finger and move right hand toward left until index finger touches back of left hand.

ARRIVE THERE Hold open left hand, palm out, in front of shoulder, and bring pointing index finger of right hand to left palm.

LOW Hold flat hand above ground at proper height.

LARGE Sign BIG. If very large, add sign for HIGH.

CORRAL   Sign TREE, and interlace fingers of both hands at first joint, as in A, to indicate logs. Then, as in B, place heels of hands together and move them apart in a semicircular motion.

HOUSE   Interlace fingers, as in A above.

FORT   Same as sign for HOUSE, but with interlaced fingers held in shape of a roof.

HAIL   Sign RAIN and COLD, and show size of hailstone.

CRAZY   Bunch tips of fingers and thumb of right hand, and hold back of hand against forehead. Rotate hand in a small circle.

ANGRY   Place closed right fist against forehead, with thumb touching head, and rotate hand, as in CRAZY. Also MAD.

IMPOSSIBLE Stab left palm with right index finger, bouncing finger back and down a little. *Meaning:* It can not go through. Also CAN NOT.

HOT Hold both hands flat above head and lower them slowly to top of head.

CARRY Hold the hands as shown, as if grasping a sack, and stoop slightly forward.

FLOUR Rub tip of right thumb against index and second finger.

BREAD Sign FLOUR, and clap hands together, right on left palm, and left on right palm, as if patting dough.

THICK Hold open left hand, palm up, and grasp the thickest part of it with the thumb and index finger of the right hand.

THIN In the same manner as above, grasp outer edge of left hand with right thumb and index finger.

WANT Place closed right hand against chin and move hand downward in a shallow arc.

THINK Hold right hand over the heart, with thumb and index finger open, other fingers closed. Move hand out, turning slightly so the back of the hand is uppermost. The Indian used this sign because he believed one thought with the heart rather than with the mind.

CRY Draw index fingers downward from corners of eyes to show flow of tears.

STOP Raise open hand, palm out. Also HALT, WAIT.

ACHE Move right index finger in a zigzag motion over aching part of the body, and sign SICK.

SICK Hold both hands open on stomach, and move them forward and backward several times.

HEADACHE Sign SICK against forehead.

TIRED Hold both hands, index fingers pointing, in front of body and a few inches apart. Then quickly drop both hands at the wrists, at the same time pulling them slightly toward the body.

EAT Move cupped right hand up and down in front of mouth.

EAT ENOUGH (FULL) Sign EAT and, with index finger and thumb spread, move right hand from chest to chin.

BACON Sign THIN and EAT.

TASTE Place tip of index finger against lips.

SWEET Sign TASTE and GOOD. Also SUGAR.

SOUR Sign TASTE and BAD. Also BITTER.

ASTONISH Quickly clasp a hand over the mouth. To show great astonishment, extend the other hand, palm out, in a warding-off motion. The facial expression should indicate great surprise, pleasure, disappointment, or fear.

FACE Draw open hand over the face from forehead to chin.

EQUAL Hold index fingers together, with hands close to body. Then, keeping hands together, move them straight ahead. Also SAME, LIKE.

ALIKE Sign FACE and EQUAL.

DARK Sign NIGHT and EQUAL.

BEAUTIFUL Sign FACE and GOOD. Also HANDSOME.

UGLY Sign FACE and BAD. Also HOMELY.

56

ASHAMED Hold hands open, backs out, at each side of face, and cross them over the face to hide it. Also **BASHFUL**.

KETTLE First, show shape of kettle with an open circle of thumbs and index fingers. Hold left hand in this position and, with the bunched fingers of the right hand, describe an arch from the tip of the left index finger to the tip of the left thumb. This is the handle of the kettle. Then make a motion of grasping the imaginary handle, as if to carry it.

LIGHT (in weight) Hold both hands in front of body, palms up, and move them up and down, as if holding a light object.

HEAVY Same position as for LIGHT, but hands are lowered quickly, as if a heavy object had just been placed in them.

BRING Hold closed right hand, with index finger pointing, well out in front of body, and draw it toward the chest, crooking the index finger.

FEAST Sign MAKE, KETTLE, TWO (or THREE), and BRING, repeating the last sign several times to indicate all directions. Then sign ALL and EAT.

FAST Hold both hands in front of body, palms facing, with left hand slightly ahead of right. Then quickly brush right palm past left palm. Also HURRY, QUICK.

GIVE Bring open right hand forward from chest as if offering something.

GIVE ME Sign GIVE, and return right hand to right shoulder.

MEET Raise both hands, fingers closed and index fingers pointing up, and bring them together until tips of index fingers meet.

ABSENT Sign SIT and NO.

SILENT Place tips of fingers against lips.

AVOID Hold hands as in sign for MEET. Then move them past each other with index fingers still pointing up. Also MISS.

ACROSS Hold left arm across body and slightly in front of it, and pass open right hand, fingers pointing forward, across left wrist. Dip right hand as it clears left arm. Also OVER, CROSS OVER.

MEAT   Place fingers of right hand against palm of left hand, and slide right hand off left a few times, as if slicing meat.

ALL GONE   Hold hands against chest, palms toward body, with right hand covering left. Change position of hands quickly, alternating left on right and right on left. Repeat several times.

DRY   Sign WATER and ALL GONE.

WITH   Hold left hand with palm facing right, and place index finger of right hand flat against left palm. Also BY, AND, BESIDE, TOGETHER.

HELP   Sign MAKE and WITH.

WHITE MAN Draw the right index finger across the forehead from left to right. This sign referred to the white man's broad-brimmed hat.

INTERPRETER Sign HE, TALK, LITTLE, WHITE MAN, and TALK.

WAGON Hold both fists close to the chest, with backs of hands down and index fingers curved. Make a forward, circular motion, as in diagram, to show turning wheels.

ROAD Sign WAGON and TRAIL.

DESTROY Brush fingers of right hand against open left hand. Also WIPE OUT.

BRIDGE Hold cupped hands together, palms up, and move them
apart horizontally. Then sign ACROSS
and RIVER.

CANOE Grasp imaginary paddle
and make paddling motions on
either side of body. Then make a
sweeping motion forward and up,
with the open right hand, to indicate the curved prow of a canoe.

BREAK Break an imaginary twig with both hands.

CANDY Sign SWEET. Then draw right index finger across
upright left index finger several times.

BLOOD Hold tips of index and
middle fingers of either hand under
nostrils, and lower the hand to chin
in a long S-motion.

EFFORT Bend slightly forward, holding fists close to each side of body. With arm muscles stiff, pull fists away from body as if moving them were a great effort. Also TRY, PUSH.

MONEY Form a complete circle with thumb and index finger.

DOLLAR Sign MONEY and ONE (or any number desired).

HALF DOLLAR Sign MONEY, and place index finger across circle.

COFFEE Hold closed right fist above left palm and make a circular motion, as if turning a crank.

TEA Sign TREE, LEAF, WATER, and GOOD.

ARISE Hold right arm close to body, with lower arm extended, palm up and index finger pointing. Then slowly raise arm until hand is even with shoulder.

AFRAID Hold right hand, index finger pointing up, in front of chest, and bring it up past face, as if drawing away.

COWARD Point to person, or sign his name, and sign AFRAID.

ABOVE Hold right hand on top of left, as shown, and raise it a few inches.

BELOW Reverse of sign for ABOVE. Hold left hand on top of right, and lower right hand a few inches.

UP (DOWN)   Point up or down.

ADD   Place palms of hands together horizontally, and raise right hand in a jerky movement, as if adding layer to layer.

HUNGRY   Move open right hand, palm up, back and forth across stomach.

COUNTRY   Point to the ground, and spread both hands low and wide.

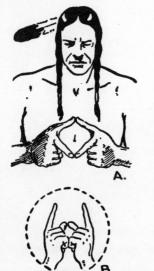

FLOWER   Sign GRASS, waist high. Then form a circle with thumbs and index fingers. Turn the fingers up, and spread them at the same time, as in B.

ROSE Pluck bunched finger tips of left hand with finger tips of right hand.

HEART Place the right hand against the heart, thumb and fingers pointing down and slightly cupped.

GENEROUS Sign HEART and BIG.

CROSS (Bad-tempered) Sign HEART and BAD.

DISGUST Sign HEART and TIRED, and look disgusted.

WISE Sign HEART. Touch forehead, and sign GOOD.

DEAF Cover right ear with palm of right hand and rub gently in a circular motion. Then sign NO.

FALL DOWN Hold right hand flat, palm down and fingers pointing to left. Then swing hand to right in a slight curve, at the same time turning hand so palm is up.

The Twelve Moons

MOON (MONTH)   Sign NIGHT, and hold right hand, palm up, toward the sky, outlining a crescent moon with the thumb and index finger. The sign for MOON is always used at the end of the description for each month.

The Indian calendar reckoned months by the moon, which waxes and wanes each 28 days. For this reason, many tribes counted 13 months in a year.

Each tribe called the months by names best suited to its own customs and region, but many of these descriptions are too long and complex for easy expression in sign language. The signs given in this book are those used by the woodland Indians. They are generally recognized by all tribes and can be used freely throughout the country.

The picture-writing symbol for each moon is shown behind the figures on pages 68-71.

JANUARY

The Snow Moon

Sign SNOW and MOON.

FEBRUARY

The Hunger Moon

Sign HUNGRY and MOON.

MARCH

The Crow Moon

Sign COLOR, BLACK,
BIRD, indicating
size of bird, and MOON.

APRIL
The Green Grass Moon

Sign COLOR, GREEN,
GRASS, and MOON.

MAY
The Planting Moon

Sign CORN, MAKE, and MOON.

JUNE
The Rose Moon

Sign ROSE and MOON.

JULY

The Thunder Moon

Sign BIRD, FIRE,
and MOON.

AUGUST

The Green Corn Moon

Sign COLOR, GREEN,
CORN, and MOON.

SEPTEMBER

The Hunting Moon

Sign HUNT and MOON.

OCTOBER

The Falling Leaf Moon

Sign LEAF and MOON.

NOVEMBER

The Mad Moon

Sign ANGRY and MOON.

DECEMBER

The Long Night Moon

Sign NIGHT, TIME, and MOON.

WATERFALL Sign RIVER. Then, holding left hand, palm down, in front of body, pass the spread fingers of the right hand over the left wrist in a wavy motion.

KNOW Hold right hand over heart, as shown, and sweep it to the right. Also **UNDERSTAND**.

KNOW NOT Sign UNDERSTAND and NO.

MEMORY Sign HEART and KNOW.

SEPARATE Place both hands together, as shown, index fingers pointing. Then flip hands over and apart.

TRUE Hold right hand close to neck, index finger pointing, and move it straight ahead. *Meaning:* Talking with a straight tongue.

ALONE Hold right hand up, index finger pointing, and move it forward in a dipping motion, as shown by the arrow.

TO Hold left hand open, palm facing right, and stab center of left palm with tip of right index finger.

SAD Sign HEART, and lower right hand toward ground. *Meaning:* My heart is on the ground.

BAG Cup left hand to indicate the open top of a bag, and pass right hand into it. Then, with both hands, indicate the size of the bag.

AWL Place right index finger across left index finger and, by wrist action, turn right index finger as if boring a hole.

BOWL Cup both hands together in a bowl shape.

FOOL Sign CRAZY and LITTLE.

DIVE Hold flat left hand open, palm facing right, and pass the open right hand down and under the left.

74

LOVE Cross arms over chest, right arm close to body, and press with the left arm. To sign FOND, use less pressure on the right arm.

OPPOSITE Hold closed hands at equal height in front of chest, index fingers pointing to each other.

ALL RIGHT Sign ALL and GOOD.

PEACE Clasp both hands together. The left hand is usually the lower hand.

KEEP Grasp the left index finger firmly with the right hand and move hands back and forth.

THUNDER Sign BIRD and FIRE. The Indians believed that the legendary Thunderbird made thunder with its flapping wings, and that lightning flashed from its eyes.

ALIVE (in the sense of being active) Hold right hand in front of chest, index finger pointing up, and make three zigzag motions away from the body.

BUY Sign MONEY and EXCHANGE.

COOK Sign MAKE and EAT.

BOIL Sign WATER and EAT. Then KETTLE and FIRE.

HALF Place edge of open right hand across knuckles of open left hand, and move right hand to right and away from left hand. Also PART OF.

KILL (HIT) Hold left hand, palm out, with index and second fingers spread to form a V. Hold right hand, index finger pointing up, at right shoulder and, with a fast, downward movement, bring right index finger into V-shaped slot of left hand.

HEAP Hold hands open near ground, palms facing each other, and bring them together. When hands are close together, shape them in a rounded curve, as if forming a small mound or heap.

LIE Place back of right hand against chin, with thumb, index, and second fingers forming arch. Then snap the fingers forward, spreading them apart at the same time, without moving hand. Repeat action. *Meaning:* Talking in two directions, or with a forked tongue.

LIAR Point to person, and sign LIE.

77

JUMP Hold back of right hand close to shoulder, with fingers bunched and pointing forward. Then move hand ahead in short, arching hops.

JOKE Place cupped hand under the chin, and move it upward in a slight curve.

RICH Sign HE, MANY, and HORSE.

CERTAIN Sign ME, KNOW, and GOOD.

LAUGH Holding elbows close to body, cup both hands and move them up and down rapidly, as if the body were shaking with laughter.

SOLDIER Hold fists in front of chest, thumbs almost touching each other, and spread them horizontally. The last motion symbolizes an army taking its position for battle.

CAVALRY Sign SOLDIER, RIDE, and HORSE.

CITY Sign HOUSE and MANY.

SHOE Sign MOCCASINS and WHITE MAN.

THIEF Point to person and sign STEAL.

WEAK Sign STRONG and NO.

COME Crook index finger of right hand and motion toward body.

SHEEP (Mountain) With bunched fingers, draw curve of ram's horns at each side of head.

SHEEP (Domestic) Sign MOUNTAIN SHEEP, WHITE MAN, and WITH.

LEAD Hold closed right hand at shoulder height, and move it forward in short, jerky movements, as if leading a pony.

BLIND Touch tips of fingers to closed eyes, and sign LOOK and NO.

GOOD EVENING Sign SUNSET, DAY, and GOOD.

GOOD MORNING Sign SUNRISE, DAY, and GOOD.

HOSPITAL Sign MEDICINE and HOUSE.

FARM Sign CORN and MAKE.

TOMORROW Sign NIGHT and DAY. Then sign SUN with left hand.

FORGET Hold open hands, palms down, in front of chest, and swing right hand across left until it strikes chest. This sign is similar to sign for NIGHT, and means "mental darkness."

HANG Hook the left index finger over the index finger of the right hand.

FLAG Raise left hand and place open right hand behind it, waving the right hand as if it were a flag.

FLOAT Sign LAKE or RIVER. Then place the right hand flat on top of the left hand, both with palms down, and move arms in a wavy motion to the right.

HAT Spread thumb and index finger across forehead, and slide hand down till fingers rest just above eyebrows.

DOCTOR Sign WHITE MAN, CHIEF, and MEDICINE.

SCHOOL (SCHOOLHOUSE) Sign WHITE MAN and HOUSE; then sign BOOK, LOOK, and KNOW.

NEGRO Sign WHITE MAN and BLACK. To the Indian, the Negro belonged to the white man's world and, therefore, he thought of him as a black white man.

THANK YOU Hold both hands shoulder high, palms facing out, and push them in a slight curve toward the person you are thanking.

TRAIN Sign WAGON, FIRE, and FAST.

STORE Sign WHITE MAN, HOUSE, and TRADE.

DRUGSTORE Sign WHITE MAN, HOUSE, MEDICINE, and TRADE.

GREAT Hold hands in front of body, palms facing body, and spread them.

GREAT SPIRIT (GOD) Sign MEDICINE and GREAT.

CHURCH Sign GREAT SPIRIT (GOD) and HOUSE.

BIBLE Sign BOOK, MEDICINE, and GREAT.

GOD BLESS YOU Hold hands, open and palms out, even with the chin. Drop them a few inches, and push them toward the person to be blessed.

AUTOMOBILE Sign WAGON. Then hold both hands as if on a steering wheel, moving them slightly to left and right.

AIRPLANE Spread both arms out like wings, and dip body to left and right. Then sign BIRD and EQUAL.

BICYCLE Sign WAGON, RIDE, SIT, and GO. In speaking of a white man riding a bicycle, the Indians say: "Lazy white man sit down and walk."

MOTION PICTURE   Sign OWL, and make cranking motion with right hand. Add sign for COLOR to indicate Technicolor.

RECORD PLAYER   Motion with right hand as if cranking a machine. Then, with the right index finger pointing down, make a flat, circular motion to show the spinning of the record and sign LISTEN and GOOD.

Counting

The Indians raised the little finger of the right hand to indicate the number ONE, and counted across the fingers from right to left. The raised little finger and ring finger of the right hand were TWO; the addition of the middle finger was THREE, etc. SIX is indicated by touching the tips of the thumbs together, while keeping the fingers of the right hand raised. For TEN, the hands are open, palms out and thumbs touching.

To show groups of tens, open and close the fingers of both hands the number of times desired up to ten tens (100).

Some tribes use another way to indicate groups of tens. Sign TEN, and draw the right index finger along one of the fingers of the left hand from the knuckle to the tip. The left thumb is TEN, the left index finger TWENTY, etc. The left little finger is FIFTY. For counting SIXTY to ONE HUNDRED, the hands are reversed, and the left index finger is drawn along each of the fingers of the right hand.

To count in HUNDREDS, sign TEN and swing the hands downward in an arc to the left. Each swing of the arc from

right to left or from left to right indicates an additional one hundred. Normally the Indians do not count high figures of more than several hundreds; instead, they would say, "The buffalo were as the blades of grass on the prairie." Many hundreds may also be indicated, however, by signing ONE HUNDRED, then holding the open left hand across the chest, palm in, and stroking it from wrist to tips of fingers with the right hand. Each stroke of the right hand represents an additional one hundred.

Indian Names and Totems

Names such as Bill, John, or Frank were unknown to the Indians. Here are some common Indian names which you may wish to use when talking sign language with your friends. The drawing beside each name is its totem, or picture-writing signature.

Boys' Names

RED CLOUD Sign CLOUD, COLOR, and RED.

MEDICINE BOY Sign MEDICINE and BOY.

RAIN-IN-THE-FACE Sign RAIN, HIT, and FACE.

RUNNING ELK Sign WALK, FAST, and ELK.

TWO ARROWS Sign the number TWO and ARROW.

TWO MOONS Sign TWO and MOON.

CRAZY HORSE Sign CRAZY and HORSE.

CRANE Sign BIRD, BIG, and WATER.

FLYING EAGLE Sign EAGLE and BIRD.

YELLOW ROBE Sign COLOR, YELLOW, and BLANKET.

RED BUFFALO Sign COLOR, RED, and BUFFALO.

TURTLE Sign WALK, WITH, and HOUSE. Then show size.

MORNING BIRD Sign MORNING and BIRD.

STRIPED WOLF Sign STRIPED and WOLF.

SNOWBIRD Sign SNOW and BIRD.

EAGLE PLUME Sign EAGLE and FEATHER.

WALKING BEAR Sign BEAR and WALK.

WADES-IN-WATER Sign WOMAN, WALK, and WATER.

MOUNTAIN FLOWER Sign MOUNTAIN and FLOWER.

MANY-SNAKE-WOMAN Sign SNAKE, MANY, and WOMAN.

OWL WOMAN Sign OWL and WOMAN.

PIPE WOMAN Sign PIPE and WOMAN.

STAR Sign STAR.

SUN WOMAN Sign SUN and WOMAN.

SINGING-LONG-TIME Sign BEFORE and SING.

SNOW OWL Sign SNOW and OWL.

MEDICINE WOMAN Sign MEDICINE and WOMAN.

Index

92

95